Technology through the Ages

AGRICULTURE
THROUGH THE AGES
From Silk to Supermarkets

MICHAEL WOODS AND MARY B. WOODS

TWENTY-FIRST CENTURY BOOKS™ / MINNEAPOLIS

For Sophie Starr

Twenty-First Century Books™
An imprint of Lerner Publishing Group, Inc.
241 First Avenue North
Minneapolis, MN 55401 USA

For reading levels and more information, look up this title at www.lernerbooks.com.

Main body text set in Bembo Std Regular
Typeface provided by Monotype Typography.

Library of Congress Cataloging-in-Publication Data

Names: Woods, Michael, 1946– author. | Woods, Mary B. (Mary Boyle), 1946– author.
Title: Agriculture through the ages : from silk to supermarkets / Michael Woods and Mary B. Woods.
Description: Minneapolis : Twenty-First Century Books, [2024] | Series: Technology through the ages | Includes bibliographical references and index. | Audience: Ages 11–18 | Audience: Grades 4–6 | Summary: "After the last ice age, humans began to settle down and grow their own food. Learn how ancient agriculture practices allowed civilizations to grow more food more efficiently and led to our modern food system"— Provided by publisher.
Identifiers: LCCN 2023011188 (print) | LCCN 2023011189 (ebook) | ISBN 9798765610060 (library binding) | ISBN 9798765625231 (paperback) | ISBN 9798765619377 (epub)
Subjects: LCSH: Agriculture—History—Juvenile literature. | Agricultural innovations— History—Juvenile literature. | Food—History—Juvenile literature. | BISAC: YOUNG ADULT NONFICTION / Cooking & Food
Classification: LCC S419 .W66 2024 (print) | LCC S419 (ebook) | DDC 338.1—dc23/ eng/20230512

LC record available at https://lccn.loc.gov/2023011188
LC ebook record available at https://lccn.loc.gov/2023011189

Manufactured in the United States of America
1 – CG – 12/15/23

CONTENTS

INTRODUCTION

What do you think of when you hear the word *technology*? You probably think of computers, smartphones, and the latest scientific tools. But technology doesn't just mean brand-new machines and discoveries. Technology is as old as human society.

Technology is the use of knowledge, inventions, and discoveries to make life better. The word technology comes from two Greek words. *Tekhne* means "art" or "craft." The suffix *-logia* means the study of arts and crafts. In modern times, technology refers to a craft, a technique, or a tool itself.

People use many kinds of technologies to treat patients, build homes and offices, and move things from place to place. This book looks at one of the technologies that has changed human life more than any other: agriculture.

Game Changer

Agriculture is the science and practice of farming. It involves raising plants and animals for food and to make other

This painting from an ancient Egyptian tomb shows a farmer cutting grain with a sickle. The tomb, near the ancient city of Thebes (modern-day Luxor), dates to the 1200s BCE. When people settled into farming villages, human society became more complex.

important materials. Growing fruits and vegetables, raising cows and sheep for milk and wool, planting trees for lumber, and raising fish for food are all examples of agriculture.

Humans were hunter-gatherers before practicing agriculture. They got food by hunting, fishing, and gathering wild plants. This lifestyle meant that hunter-gatherers had to move from place to place so they did not overhunt or overfish an area.

Ancient people invented agriculture around twelve thousand years ago. It had a huge impact on how early people lived. Farming allowed them to settle down and live

in one place where they could raise animals and grow crops year after year. This gave them more control over the food they ate. Often they could grow more food than they could find hunting or gathering. Eventually, some small farming settlements grew into towns. Towns grew into cities. With better agriculture, many people in big cities could work in non-farming jobs. Society in these cities became more complex. People could focus on toolmaking, medicine, art, or government. In this way, agriculture helped change the course of early human history.

Beginnings

Some of the first farmers on Earth lived in a region called the Fertile Crescent. This was a crescent-shaped area of rich soil in the ancient Middle East. The Fertile Crescent stretched through parts of modern-day Israel, Lebanon, Syria, Turkey, and Iraq. People there began farming around 10,000 BCE. A few thousand years later, people in what are now China, India, and the Americas began farming. Gradually, farming spread to most parts of the world.

Agriculture and Archaeologists

The first farmers left many clues about their agricultural technology. Some made pictures of farming, farm animals, and food processing. After the invention of writing, people left us written accounts of agriculture.

Archaeologists also learn about ancient farming practices by studying the tools people used to prepare food. They have found ancient knives for cutting meat, stones for grinding

Ancient peoples made many of the same foods modern people prepare. This carving from an ancient tomb in Saqqara, Egypt, shows bakers making bread. The carving dates to around 2400 BCE.

grain, containers for carrying food, and ovens for baking bread. Sometimes archaeologists even find remains of ancient food. These include ancient pots with food smudges or stains inside. Archaeologists can test those remains to identify the kind of food they stored in the pot.

A Lot with a Little

Ancient farmers did not have tractors or other motorized equipment to help them plow, plant, and harvest crops. There were no factories to process and preserve food. Instead, they had to use trial and error to find more effective crops and growing methods. They bred farm animals to produce offspring that gave more milk or had more wool. They found ways to keep food from spoiling. They invented ways of using farm products in new ways. Milk and wheat, for instance, were turned into cheese and bread. Grapes and olives became wine and olive oil. Read on and discover how this ancient technology led to modern supermarkets with thousands of different delicious foods.

CHAPTER ONE

Before Agriculture

The first humans lived about three hundred thousand years ago. Early humans fished in lakes, rivers, and oceans. They hunted and trapped animals. They gathered wild, edible plants such as nuts, acorns, grains, berries, and fruits. Sometimes they hunted herds of wild animals, following them from place to place.

Hunter-gatherers were also scavengers. If they found dead meat on the ground, they may have eaten it. Early humans competed with vultures and hyenas for these scraps of bone and meat. If a lion left bones from his antelope meal, our ancestors could use stones to crack open the bones and eat the rich marrow inside.

Before the invention of agriculture, people could not be picky about their food. They had to eat whatever was available. They did not have the stable supply of food many people have today. Sometimes they could not find plants to gather or game to hunt. Drought, wildfire, or extreme weather killed plants and animals over large areas. By developing new technologies, ancient peoples could preserve

and store supplies of food to eat in hard times. Eventually, they could be pickier and supply more nutritious and tastier food.

Prehistoric Technology

Over the centuries, humans developed new tools for hunting and gathering. They invented spears and bows and arrows for killing animals. They crafted nets and traps for snaring fish and game. Wooden shovels to dig into the soil have been used since at least 3,700 BCE.

At first, hunter–gatherers ate only raw foods. About 300,000 BCE, people in Europe began to use fire to cook food. Cooking makes food easier to chew and helps the body absorb more nutrients. It also makes certain foods taste better

Animal bones contain nutritious bone marrow. Ancient hunter-gatherers split these bones in half so they could eat the marrow inside.

and destroys harmful substances in some foods. For instance, the plant cassava contains cyanide, which can be deadly if eaten. But cooking cassava removes the poison. After ancient peoples in South America learned to cook cassava, it became a mainstay of their diet.

Another benefit of cooking is that it can kill harmful microbes in food. These invisible organisms, such as bacteria and viruses, can sometimes make people sick. Early peoples did not know about these advantages of cooking, but they knew that eating cooked food tasted better, was easier to chew, and was safer to eat.

Something Fishy

Hunter-gatherers used animal bones, wood, and antlers to make fishing spears. Early humans who lived in ancient Europe between thirty-five thousand and ten thousand years ago made barbed fishing spears. Barbs are backward-facing points on a spearhead or an arrowhead. A fish can easily slip off an ordinary spearhead. But a barbed spearhead will catch in a fish's flesh, making escape difficult.

Early humans also made fishhooks from curved pieces of wood, bone, or shell. Fishing lines attached to the hooks were probably made from vine or woven plant fibers, but these have rotted away over time. Ancient fishers may have baited the hooks with worms or insects. Tomb paintings in Egypt show that people three thousand years ago were using a similar technology, the fishing net.

The first fishhooks were J-shaped. They caught fish only when the hooks wedged securely in a fish's mouth or gills. Fish were often able to wiggle out of those hooks. Around

This prehistoric carving of a salmon was found in a cave in France. Coastal peoples relied on fishing for much of their food.

5000 BCE, people in ancient Scandinavia (modern-day Denmark, Norway, and Sweden) invented barbed fishhooks. Like barbed spearheads, barbed fishhooks have points that project backward. The barb helps fishhooks stick firmly in place.

Containers

Hunter-gatherers needed containers to hold the fruits, nuts, and roots they collected. At first, people used natural objects as containers. They stored and carried food in dried gourds and big seashells. Ancient peoples also sewed animal skins for bags. Later, ancient peoples used reeds, leaves, bark, and other plant fibers to weave baskets.

Hunter-gatherers in Japan made the world's first known clay container around 14,000 BCE. The round-bottomed pot was found at an ancient site in northern Honshu, the main

island of Japan. Within a few thousand years, people in other ancient cultures learned to make pottery. The process was simple. People shaped wet clay into bowls and other vessels. First, they dried the vessels in the sun. Later, people heated pottery in kilns, or ovens. This process made the vessels stronger and more watertight.

Domestication

Domesticating wild animals was a major advance in agriculture. Domestication is similar to taming. Domesticated

Early peoples domesticated animals for many reasons. Donkeys, oxen, and horses could carry heavy loads and pull vehicles. Cows provided milk, meat, and leather. Chickens gave people eggs. Dogs were good hunters and guard animals. This stone carving, from around 2000 BCE, shows an ancient Egyptian with a hunting dog.

Food Preservation

Early humans also needed ways to keep food from spoiling. By studying ancient fish bones, archaeologists know that ancient hunter-gatherers sometimes smoked fish to preserve it. They hung fish over smoky fires. Chemicals in wood smoke can slow the growth of bacteria and other microbes that cause food to spoil.

In cold weather, ancient peoples stored food in snow and ice. This slowed or stopped the growth of microbes, just like fridges and freezers. Ancient peoples often dried food in the sun or over fires. Drying removes moisture that microbes need to grow.

animals live among people instead of in the wild. This gave ancient peoples easier access to meat, eggs, milk, and fur. Instead of hunting wild pigs for days on end, ancient people could simply catch one from their pig pen.

Archaeologists think that people in the Middle East domesticated dogs more than twelve thousand years ago. At first, people probably kept wild dogs near their camps as watchdogs. Dogs scared away human and animal attackers, killed snakes, and kept mice and rats from eating stored food. People fed the dogs to keep them nearby. Dogs also accompanied hunters. With their excellent sense of smell, dogs were good at tracking game.

Gradually, people realized that they could breed dogs with the most desirable qualities. For instance, a hunter might mate their best hunting dogs. Their offspring would likely also be good hunters. Generations of such breeding changed

the nature and appearance of dogs. It created new breeds with different traits. Many of the same changes occurred in other domesticated animals.

Settling Down

Around the same time that people domesticated animals, they also began to domesticate plants. Instead of searching for wild plants to eat, ancient peoples began saving and collecting seeds. Crops could be grown closer to their homes. As a result, people began living in the same place and harvesting the same fields year after year.

Agriculture transformed human society in countless ways. Once they were settled in one place, people built permanent homes. Sometimes farmers grew more food than their families could eat. They sold or traded the surplus. These transactions led people to develop record-keeping systems, writing, and currency. People also built roads and more complicated vehicles to carry goods from place to place.

Some small farm settlements grew to become big cities. As society within these cities became more complicated, people devoted more time to art, learning, and technology. They established laws and systems of government. In this way, farming led to the development of complex ancient societies.

Farming was hard work. Early farmers still had to worry about drought and disease, just as hunter-gatherers did. But farming was often a more reliable method of obtaining food than hunting and gathering. With the start of agriculture, Earth's human population nearly doubled. In 10,000 BCE, Earth had fewer than 3 million people. By 8000 BCE, the human population was 5.3 million. The changes caused by

Ancient peoples got wool, meat, and milk from domesticated sheep. This Roman sarcophagus shows a shepherd tending sheep in ancient Italy.

farming were so amazing that historians refer to them as the agricultural revolution.

Prehistoric Refrigerators

In ancient North America, early peoples hunted mammoths. These giant animals, the relatives of modern elephants, contained thousands of pounds of meat. That was good news for hungry hunter-gatherers. But a small band of hunter-gatherers could not eat all the meat from a mammoth at once. So these ancient people devised ways to keep the meat from spoiling.

Ancient hunters probably used snow and ice, smoking, and drying to preserve meat. But University of Michigan professor Daniel Fisher thinks they might have used another method as well. Fisher thinks that ancient hunter-gatherers used a technology called underwater caching (storage).

Underwater caching involves sinking chunks of meat into lakes and ponds. Underwater, cold temperatures, helpful bacteria, and low levels of oxygen keep the meat from rotting. Fisher discovered butchered mammoth bones at the bottom of lakes in the Great Lakes region of the United States. The bones suggested that ancient North Americans used underwater caching to preserve mammoth meat eleven thousand years ago.

To prove his theory, Fisher and two coworkers performed an experiment. In winter they dropped pieces of lamb, deer, and horsemeat into the bottom of a pond. They also stored control, or comparison, samples in a modern freezer. The researchers periodically tested samples in a laboratory. After several months, they found the cached meat was just as fresh as the meat stored in the freezer.

CHAPTER TWO
The Ancient Middle East

E arth has gone through many ice ages. These are long periods of cold temperatures when much of the land, especially in the northern hemisphere, was covered with sheets of ice. The most recent ice age ended around 11,000 BCE. Afterwards, enormous fields of wild wheat, barley, and other grains began to grow in the Fertile Crescent. Hunter-gatherers in that area began to rely on this wild grain for food. At first they probably just collected kernels of wild grain. People cooked the grain or ground it up to make flour.

Slowly, the hunter-gatherer lifestyle began to change in the Fertile Crescent and other parts of the ancient Middle East. People settled down to grow grain and raise animals. After many years, these farming peoples began to organize themselves. They created towns, laws, and economic systems.

One part of the Fertile Crescent was called Mesopotamia, which means "between rivers" in ancient Greek. Mesopotamia was between the Tigris and Euphrates Rivers centered in modern-day Iraq. It was home to several ancient societies, including the Sumerians, Assyrians, and Babylonians.

Goats and Sheep

Wild goats and sheep were abundant in the hills of the ancient Middle East. By domesticating these animals, early Middle Eastern farmers obtained milk, meat, and wool. Because these animals have strong herding instincts, they were easier to domesticate than other animals. They tend to stay in groups and follow lead animals. They rarely try to run away.

Ancient Middle Eastern farmers learned to breed animals with desirable traits. If a farmer wanted big, even-tempered sheep that gave lots of milk, the farmer mated animals with those characteristics. The sheep that were small, aggressive, or poor milk producers might be butchered for meat. Over

This Sumerian panel from Ur, Mesopotamia, shows a banquet with a cow and a sheep. The panel is made of wood, lapis lazuli (a semiprecious stone), and shell and dates to 3000 to 2340 BCE.

several generations of sheep, this led to herds of large, docile sheep that gave lots of milk.

The Plow

Plows loosen or turn over soil to make long furrows, or trenches, in a field. Farmers place seeds in these trenches so their plants grow in orderly lines. Plowing also helps control weeds and insect pests. Archaeologists think ancient Middle Eastern farmers made the first plows soon after they began farming.

Farmers might have made the first plows from forked tree branches. Farmers used the forked end of the branch as a double handle. They sharpened the opposite end into a point. Pushing or pulling the sharp point through the soil loosened it. People soon realized that a plow works better if one person steers it while an animal does the pulling.

Oxen were ideal for pulling plows. They could plow more land in one day than a farmer could do in a whole week. The first known picture of an ox comes from ancient Turkey around 6500 BCE. The oldest pictures of oxen hitched to plows date to around 3000 BCE in Egypt and Mesopotamia.

Ancient peoples improved plows by adding moldboards

This stone carving from ancient Assyria shows a man hoisting water with a shadoof.

to the front. These curved wood or metal plates dug neat furrows. They also lifted and turned the soil. In the process, moldboards removed weeds from the field. Moldboards also churned up nutrient-rich soil from belowground, creating a fertile planting layer on top.

Moving Water

Watering crops was hard work for ancient farmers. One gallon (3.8 L) of water weighs about 8 pounds (3.6 kg). Some ancient fields may have needed thousands of gallons of water each day.

To make this job easier, people in Mesopotamia invented the shadoof. A shadoof is a long pole with a bucket on one end. It has a fulcrum, or pivot point, in the center, and a weight on the other end. The shadoof acted as a lever, allowing farmers to easily lift a heavy bucket of water from a river or lake. Farmers used shadoofs to hoist water from rivers and more easily irrigate their crops. They poured the water directly onto crops or into storage tanks. The first picture of an ancient shadoof comes from Mesopotamia. It was carved on clay and dates to around 2300 BCE.

Pottery

People in the ancient Middle East learned to make pottery after they began farming. These peoples needed containers to hold water, milk, wine, olive oil, and other foods. At first, Middle Eastern potters shaped pots by hand. They often used the coiling method—winding long strands of clay to make the walls of a pot. Sometimes they scooped out the center of lumps of clay to make simple bowls.

Royal Purple

Ancient people in the Middle East made dyes from plants, minerals, and animal secretions. They used the dyes to color clothing and other textiles. The ancient Phoenicians, in modern-day Lebanon, made a beautiful purple dye. They called it Tyrian purple, after the Phoenician seaport of Tyre. The dye came from the glands of a shellfish. Rare and costly, Tyrian purple became a symbol of royalty and wealth in the ancient world.

Tyrian purple and other dyes presented a challenge for ancient Middle Eastern cloth makers. The wool of the first domesticated sheep was grayish brown. Such dark fabric wasn't good for dyeing. Dye doesn't show up on dark wool. To make colored fabric, a clothing maker needed white wool. So shepherds needed to raise sheep with white coats. They solved this problem by mating male and female sheep with light coats. Their offspring also had light coats. By 1000 BCE, this practice had led to sheep with white wool, which took dye well. This same breeding technology also led to pre-colored wool. It produced sheep that grew black or gray wool that didn't require dye.

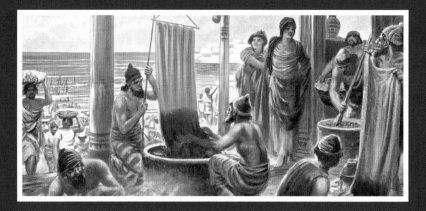

This illustration by the artist Ambrose Dudley shows what the ancient process of dye making might have looked like.

This pottery vessel has a spout, so it was probably used for carrying and pouring liquid. It comes from ancient Iraq and dates to around 2500 BCE.

Around 3500 BCE, people in Mesopotamia made an important advancement in pottery production. They invented the potter's wheel. The wheel was a rotating wooden disk. The potter placed a lump of wet clay in the center. They turned the wheel by hand while coiling or pinching the walls of the pot. The turning wheel allowed the potter to build the walls more evenly and faster than could be done by hand alone.

Ancient Mesopotamian potters hardened clay vessels by heating or "firing" them in kilns. They also learned to coat pots with certain minerals before firing them. When heated, the minerals formed a glaze, or waterproof coating.

23

The First Fabrics

Domesticated animals produced more than food. Some were used to make other products such as clothing. Fibers made from plants including cotton, flax, and hemp can be turned into fabrics for clothes. Animal fiber, such as sheep's wool or camel hair, can also be turned into fabric. People in the ancient Middle East used all these fibers to make fabric.

Turning fibers into fabric involves several kinds of technology. One is spinning. Most natural fibers are very short. Cotton fibers, for instance, are only about 0.5 inches (1.3 cm) long. Spinning changes short pieces of fiber into long strands of thread or yarn.

Mesopotamians used tools called spindles and distaffs to turn fiber into yarn. A distaff is a small stick with a slot on one end. The slot holds clumps of fiber. A spindle is a long straight stick held between the thumb and the index finger. By twirling the spindle, a person carefully draws fibers off the distaff. The short fibers cling and twist together. They become a long strand of yarn.

The next step in making fabric is weaving. This craft involves interlacing two strands of thread or yarn at right angles. You can see this pattern yourself by looking through a magnifying glass at the tiny threads in cotton cloth. Weavers use a loom to hold the two sets of strands. Ancient Middle Eastern weavers used simple hand-operated looms. These small wooden frames kept one set of threads (the warp) pulled tight while the weaver interlaced the crosswise threads (the weft).

People have also made clothes from felt for thousands of years. Felt can be made without spinning or weaving. It

Agriculture includes more than growing and preparing food. Making fabric is also part of agricultural technology. This terra-cotta tablet from ancient Babylon shows a person using a loom to weave cloth. The tablet dates from the second millennium BCE.

This stone relief from the fifth century BCE depicts Medes (ancient Iranians) wearing felt caps.

is made from compressed wool fibers, locked together in a dense tangle. Felt forms naturally in the coats of sheep that are molting, or shedding. People can also turn loose wool into felt by wetting or heating the wool and pressing the fibers together. Felt was an important fabric in the ancient Middle East. People used it to make clothing, especially heavy garments for cold weather. The ancient Persians, based in modern-day Iran, made felt caps with earflaps. Felt is still used as a warm lining for winter boots.

Ancient Spirits

Alcoholic drinks were common in the ancient world. Archaeologists have found beer residue inside a clay jar from Mesopotamia. The jar, dated from between 3500 and 3100 BCE. It was marked with the ancient Mesopotamian symbol for beer.

"Again you will plant vineyards on the hills of Samaria [modern-day Israel and Jordan]; the farmers will plant them and enjoy their fruit."

—Hebrew Bible, first millennium BCE

Wine was also popular in the ancient Middle East. Researchers at the University of Pennsylvania Museum of Archaeology and Anthropology in Philadelphia examined yellowish wine residue inside two ancient jars from northern Iran. Tests showed that the jars were made between about 5400 and 5000 BCE. They are the world's oldest known wine jars.

But even these aren't the oldest known beer or wine bottles. In 2004 researchers at the same museum in Philadelphia examined ancient pottery jars from China. Tests revealed that the jars had held an alcoholic drink made from rice, fruit, and honey. The jars were made sometime between 7000 to 6600 BCE.

To make alcoholic beverages, ancient peoples used fermentation. During this process, bacteria, yeast, and other microbes make chemical changes to food. For example, fermentation can change grape juice into wine. It can also change mashed grain into beer and milk into cheese and yogurt.

CHAPTER THREE
Ancient Egypt

The Nile is often considered the world's longest river. It flows from central Africa north to Egypt and the Mediterranean Sea. More than seven thousand years ago, ancient hunter-gatherers began to settle in Egypt around the Nile. People built permanent farms along the river. They grew wheat and other crops. Before long, a complex society had developed in ancient Egypt.

Every year, heavy rains fall in central Africa. In ancient times, these rains flooded the Nile. The floodwaters soaked the dry soil. When the waters receded in autumn, they left behind muddy silt, or sediment. The silt was full of nutrients perfect for growing crops.

Agricultural technology made the ancient Egyptians one of the world's greatest wheat producers. They farmed wheat fields with oxen, plows, and other tools. Egyptian farmers also grew cotton, millet (a kind of grain), and flax, which was woven into linen. Egyptian shepherds raised goats and sheep, and farmers raised pigs.

The soil surrounding the Nile River is extremely fertile. This rich soil enabled ancient Egyptian farmers to grow wheat, millet, and other grains.

Irrigation

Around 3100 BCE, a ruler named Menes united the people of Egypt under one government. He established Egypt's first dynasty, or ruling family. After unifying Egypt, King Menes built irrigation systems. Irrigation involves supplying water to crops to improve yields. It involves damming rivers, digging canals, building ponds, and other measures for moving, storing, and controlling water. Irrigated farmland yields much more food per acre than nonirrigated farmland. About 2300 BCE, the Egyptians dug a 12-mile (19 km) canal from the Nile to Lake

This painting shows Egyptian farmers harvesting crops and tending farm animals. The original painting, made around 1400 BCE, is in a tomb near modern-day Luxor. The picture shown here is a copy, made in the twentieth century by artist Nina Davies. Her copies of this and other tomb paintings have made it easier for scholars to study them.

Moeris. When the Nile flooded, water flowed through the canal to the lake. The lake served as a storage tank for the excess river water. Farmers used the water for year-round irrigation.

Wine and Beer

Wine and beer making were big business in ancient Egypt. At first, ancient Egyptians imported wine from modern-day Lebanon and Israel. Then Egyptian farmers began to import grapevines from the same places. This allowed them to grow their own grapes and make their own wine. Starting around

3000 BCE, Egyptian rulers oversaw large-scale wine-making operations. A wall painting from 1400 BCE from the Egyptian city of Thebes shows two men picking grapes. Other men tread on a vat of grapes to make juice. The painting also shows amphorae, pottery jars for fermenting grape juice into wine. The ancient Egyptians buried their kings in treasure-filled tombs. King Tutankhamen, who died around 1324 BCE, was buried with twenty-six jugs of red and white wine, in addition to many other luxuries.

The Top Farmer

When ancient Egyptians paid taxes to the government, they did not use money. They sent sacks of nuts and grains to the vizier, a high-ranking government official. They also paid with livestock. The government stockpiled that extra food. If famine (widespread hunger) struck, the government used its stockpiles to feed hungry people.

CHAPTER FOUR
Ancient China

Rice has long been an important crop in China. Rice farming in China began more than eight thousand years ago in the Yangtze River valley. Wild rice grew throughout this area. Chinese hunter-gatherers gradually learned to save and plant rice seeds.

Because the soil in the Yangtze Valley was wet and heavy, ancient Chinese rice farmers needed sturdy tools. They used strong shovels to dig into the soil. The shovels had wooden handles and blades made from the shoulder bones of buffalo.

But rice was not the first grain domesticated there. About nine thousand years ago, farmers in northern China domesticated millet. They then domesticated wheat, soybeans, barley, and other grains.

Puddling Rice

The first Chinese farmers probably planted rice seeds directly into the soil. But this approach posed problems. The rice seeds grew into mature plants, as expected. But weeds tended to

Modern Chinese farmers still use flooded rice fields. They are terraced, or cut into a series of levels. Terracing allows farmers to grow crops on hilly terrain. Ancient Chinese farmers used rice fields like these fourteen hundred years ago.

spring up along with the rice plants. Farmers needed to weed their fields often. And rice plants need a lot of water. During wet years, Chinese rice crops flourished. But crops suffered during dry weather.

Around 800 BCE, Chinese farmers came up with a solution to the weed and water problems. They began to transplant rice seedlings into paddies, or flooded fields. Called puddling, it produced a better crop. In flooded fields, rice plants got plenty of water, even during dry spells. And weeds couldn't grow in flooded fields.

Puddling improved the rice crop in ancient China, but it required specialized irrigation systems. Farmers had to build irrigation canals to carry water to their fields and barriers to

Chrysanthemums contain a chemical called pyrethrum that repels and kills some insects but does not harm people. Ancient Chinese farmers used the flowers to keep insects from eating their crops. We still use that natural chemical today.

keep the water in the fields. They also built control gates to let water in and out of fields as necessary.

Biological Pest Control

Insects, fungi, rodents, and other pests destroy nearly a third of all the crops people plant worldwide. Pests were a big problem for ancient farmers as well.

Modern farmers often use poisonous chemicals to kill insects and other crop pests. In ancient China, farmers used a more natural method to kill insects. They used biological pest control. It involves killing pests with their own natural enemies. Often these enemies are other insects. For instance, praying mantises eat other bugs that can destroy plants. In ancient China, farmers released praying mantises into their flower and vegetable fields.

In parts of ancient China, it was illegal to kill frogs.

That's because frogs ate huge amounts of insects that damaged crops. Chinese fruit farmers hung burning torches in tree branches. The firelight attracted insects, which burned up when they reached the flames. Around 100 CE, the Chinese began to use chrysanthemums for biological pest control. Farmers dried the flowers and ground them into a fine powder. The powder killed insects on vegetable plants but did not harm other animals or people.

Some farmers in ancient China grew mandarin oranges. Like modern consumers, Chinese shoppers wanted flawless fruit for their money. They didn't want oranges damaged by fungus or filled with wormholes. Ancient Chinese fruit growers used yellow citrus killer ants to protect their oranges from pests. Growers released the ants into their orange trees. They sometimes built little bamboo bridges from tree to tree to help ants spread throughout the groves.

Pearl Makers

Farming fish, shrimp, clams, and other water animals is called aquaculture. But one kind of aquaculture does not produce food. It produces precious gems: pearls.

Pearls come from oysters. These shellfish form pearls when a foreign substance, such as a bit of sand, enters its shell. The foreign material irritates the oyster, much like a speck of dirt can irritate a person's eye. In response to the irritation, the oyster secretes layers of nacre, or mother-of-pearl. This shiny material coats the irritant. Then nacre hardens to become a pearl.

The ancient Chinese were the first known pearl farmers. They started by collecting oysters and checking them for pearls that grew naturally. To get more pearls, the ancient Chinese

Ancient Eating Utensils

People in China started using chopsticks around 3000 BCE. These two long, thin sticks allow people to pick up food without getting messy or burning their fingers. People use them by pinching food between the sticks. The first chopsticks were probably made from twigs. People later made chopsticks from bamboo stems, animal bones, animal tusks, and metal. From China, chopsticks spread to other parts of Asia.

began deliberately putting sand and other material into oysters' shells. These deliberately made pearls are called cultured pearls.

People in the ancient world valued pearls just as modern people do. Wealthy women wanted to wear pearl earrings and necklaces. Chinese merchants made a lot of money by selling pearls to people in other ancient lands.

Growing Side by Side

Most ancient farmers raised a variety of crops and animals. Some ancient Chinese farmers even raised plants and animals together. At least twelve thousand years ago, they began raising fish in the same flooded fields they used to grow rice or other crops.

Rice is one of the few crops that grow well in flooded soil. Chinese farmers flooded their rice paddies, or fields, to stop weeds from growing. Then the ancient Chinese farmers added carp to the paddies. When the carp pooped, this became manure that mixed into the water and soil. The manure fertilized the soil. It added nutrients to it that rice needs to grow.

In this ancient Chinese stone carving, a man cuts up a fish with a knife. Another man hauls in a catch of fish, while more fish hang from a line.

The carp manure also made it easy for water plants called plankton to grow. The carp ate that plankton and continued to grow. The carp also ate weeds and insects, which otherwise would have damaged the rice crops. The tall rice plants, in turn, provided shelter for the carp. Both rice and carp helped each other. This is called a symbiotic relationship. Ancient farmers used this relationship to harvest and sell both the carp and rice.

Animal manure is a natural and common fertilizer. Since ancient times, farmers have used manure from their own livestock to fertilize farmlands. Farmers have also used human feces, or poop, and human urine as fertilizer for thousands of years. Those materials are still used in some parts of the world.

Domesticating the Silkworm

The ancient Chinese raised many kinds of farm animals. Some Chinese farmers even raised silkworms. Silkworms are the caterpillar form of the silkworm moth. People have long prized this insect for the fabric that is made from its cocoon, silk. Silk is extremely strong and lightweight.

People in ancient China wanted long silk fibers to make silk fabric. They developed a technique to get silk fibers from cocoons before silkworm moths emerged and broke the long fibers. Silkworm farmers collected the eggs of silkworm moths. When the eggs hatched, silk growers let them feast on the leaves of mulberry trees. After four or five weeks, the silkworms spun their cocoons on twigs or pieces of straw. Before the silkworm moths could burst out of their cocoons, farmers heated the cocoons in ovens or boiled them in water to kill the insects inside. Silk farmers then boiled the cocoons to remove the sticky substance holding the silk in place. They unwound the silk strands from the cocoons and twisted them together to form thread. The silk thread was then woven into fabric. Modern silkworm farmers still do this.

Each silkworm cocoon contains only a small amount of silk. It takes about twenty-seven hundred silkworms to make 1 pound (0.5 kg) of silk fabric. This makes silk very expensive. In ancient Rome, silk fabric cost as much as an equal weight of gold.

Ancient Chinese stories say that the Empress Leizu discovered silk around 2700 BCE. One story says she was drinking hot tea under a mulberry tree when a cocoon fell into her cup. She watched it unwind into silk threads. Then she started the first silkworm farm. The ancient Chinese kept the

silk-making process a carefully guarded secret. Since no one outside China knew how to make silk, people in other countries had to buy their silk from China.

Around 300 CE, people in Japan and India discovered the secret. They began producing their own silk. But people farther west still didn't know how to make it. They continued to pay high prices for silk from Japan, India, and China. In about 550, Justinian I, head of the Byzantine Empire, sent two monks on a spying mission to China. The monks learned the secret of silk making. They hid mulberry seeds and silkworm eggs inside their walking staffs, and brought them back to Constantinople (modern-day Istanbul, Turkey). Silk-making technology spread from Constantinople to Europe.

Ancient Snow Cones

The story of ice cream's invention begins almost four thousand years ago in ancient China. The Chinese began using snow from the mountains to make a treat much like modern frozen rice pudding. The pudding consisted of mashed rice, milk, and spices. They froze jars of the mixture by packing them in snow. Later, the Chinese mixed snow with fruit juices to make the world's first snow cones. People in Italy discovered these treats in the 1300s CE. A few hundred years later, a Spanish physician living in Italy adapted this process to make ice cream. It involved putting the ingredients inside a small container. That container went into a larger container filled with ice, snow, and saltpeter (a kind of mineral). The saltpeter made the ice and snow even colder, freezing the ingredients in the inner container. Mixtures that contained milk or cream became the first modern ice cream.

CHAPTER FIVE
The Ancient Americas

The first people probably arrived in North America about thirty thousand years ago. That's about fifteen thousand years earlier than many historians used to think. They came from Siberia in modern-day Russia. One theory claimed that humans walked across a land bridge that once linked Siberia and modern-day Alaska. Ocean levels were lower then. Another theory suggests that ancient peoples sailed from Siberia, staying close to the coast of the Pacific Ocean. After sailing over open stretches of water, they camped on the shore. They needed to rest and get food and fresh water. No matter how they arrived, these newcomers were hunter-gatherers. They probably followed herds of animals deeper into North America.

Ancient Americans slowly moved south through modern-day Canada. They reached the American Great Plains, modern-day Mexico, and Central America. Scientists once thought that humans arrived at the tip of South America about twelve thousand years ago. But new evidence suggests that it happened at least three thousand years earlier.

In ancient Aztec culture, Yacatecuhtli was the god of trade. In this painting, he carries maize, or corn, in his hand and on his back. Corn was an important food for people throughout much of the ancient Americas.

Food First

Our information about ancient Americans' food and agriculture comes from artifacts, things they made and left behind. These include grinding stones, irrigation ditches, tools, and containers for holding food. Some ancient American artists made paintings on rocks and the stone walls of caves. Others carved shapes in rocks. These include images of corn gods and people harvesting crops and preparing food. In the late 1400s, European explorers began to arrive in the Americas. They wrote about the peoples

41

People in many ancient cultures prayed to food gods, asking for a good harvest. This sculpture depicts the Mayan corn god. It comes from the palace of Yax Pac, a Mayan king, and dates to around 775 CE.

they encountered. Some of these writings describe agriculture.

Experts think that ancient Americans first began to grow crops eight to ten thousand years ago. In Mexico people grew corn, squash, and beans. In the Andes Mountains of South America, people domesticated beans, potatoes, and the grain quinoa.

When ancient Americans settled down and began to

grow crops, they also built villages. Some villages became big cities, eventually leading to complex civilizations and empires. Mexico and Central America were home to many large ancient civilizations. These included first the Maya, then the Toltec, and later the Aztecs. In the Andes Mountains of South America, a series of civilizations rose over many thousands of years. The last and most well-known of these was the Inca Empire, which expanded from the city of Cuzco in the 1400s CE.

The original occupants of the Americas north of modern-day Mexico did not build such empires. Most of them continued to live in small groups of hunter-gatherers. However, here were exceptions. One was the Pueblos, who lived in today's southwestern United States. They were farmers. Like peoples in ancient Mexico and Central America, they mostly grew corn, squash, and beans.

Beans with Bad Valves

Domesticating plants is much like domesticating animals. People save seeds from plants with the most desirable traits and planted them. Then they save and plant the seeds from the new plants. After many generations, domesticated plants become very different from their wild ancestors.

The story of domesticated beans shows this process in action. The modern-day common bean, Phaseolus vulgaris, comes in many varieties. These include black beans, kidney beans, and pinto beans. All these beans have a common wild ancestor. It grew in ancient South and Central America.

When a wild bean plant matured, its pods opened. Each pod split into two valves, or halves, and ejected edible seeds.

43

This system was good for the bean. It was nature's way of spreading bean seeds and making sure they grew into new plants each season. But the system was inefficient for ancient Americans. Seeds often shot out of bean pods before anyone could collect them. If ancient Americans wanted to grow beans, they had to collect pods with "bad valves." Those were pods that didn't split easily or at all.

Ancient farmers in South and Central America collected these pods and saved the beans for planting. Many of the beans grew into plants that also had bad valves. Their seeds stayed in the bean pods until harvesttime. Then people collected the pods and opened them to collect the beans. This practice of harvesting and planting beans with bad pod valves eventually gave us modern common beans.

Fire and Water

From about 400 BCE to 900 CE, the Maya lived in what is now southern Mexico. The land was heavily forested. To clear space for farming, the Maya used slash-and-burn agriculture. Using stone axes, they chopped down trees in a section of forest. After the wood dried out, the farmers set the field on fire. Burning cleared the land and left a layer of ash on the soil. This ash provided nutrients for crops.

On the newly cleared land, Maya farmers planted corn, beans, and squash. But after a few years of planting, the soil in the field began to grow less fertile. So farmers moved on to slash, burn, and plant another area of forest. They would then let the land lie fallow, or unused, for a few years. Leaving the soil alone in this way allows more nutrients to form, making the soil more fertile and productive. The farmers would

A Balanced Meal

The Maya knew that corn, beans, and squash grew well together. The Maya also ate these three foods together in one meal. In doing so, they happened upon a nearly perfect food combination. Both beans and corn are healthful foods on their own. But neither contains the full variety of amino acids that the human body needs. Amino acids are essential to good health because they help the body make proteins. Corn is low in lysine but is especially rich in another amino acid, methionine. Beans are rich in lysine but low in methionine. Eaten together, beans and corn provide the body with all essential amino acids. Squash provides vitamins and minerals that humans need but are lacking in corn and beans.

return to farm again after more nutrients had entered the soil. This is similar to modern farming farm rotation, which involves planting fields with different crops from year to year and then leaving the field fallow to recover.

Central America and southern Mexico have a wet or rainy season from June to October and a dry season from November to May. During the wet season, rain often falls daily. Ancient Maya farmers needed to save some rainwater from the wet season for the dry season. They let rainwater collect in artificial ponds and underground chambers that served as reservoirs, or storage ponds. They also built irrigation channels and small dams, which helped them move water to and from reservoirs. Where the land was swampy with too much water, Maya farmers dug drainage ditches to dry it out.

After digging irrigation ditches, the Maya sometimes piled the dug-up soil between two ditches. They grew crops on top of the piles. They also dredged nutrient-rich muck from the bottom of the irrigation ditches and used it as fertilizer. Maya farmers covered crops with layers of leaves. The mulch helped keep the soil from drying out.

Modern farmers sometimes plant cover crops like clover or alfalfa. These are crops that cover the soil where other plants are being grown as well to manage erosion and keep the soil nutrient-rich. Maya farmers used a variation of cover crops. They planted corn and beans in the same fields. That way, the beans restored the nitrogen that the corn plants removed. Maya farmers also planted squash among the corn and beans. Squash grows close to the ground. It doesn't compete with bean plants, which grow higher. Squash's big flat leaves also help keep the ground covered, shaded, and moist with its large, flat leaves. This process, called companion planting, is still used.

Agriculture in the Andes

Before they settled down to farm, ancient Andeans hunted wild animals called guanacos and vicuñas. Both are related to camels. Gradually, the ancient Andeans domesticated and bred both animals. Guanacos became llamas. These long-eared animals stand 3 to 4 feet (0.9 to 1.2 m) high at the shoulder. They have long, thick wool. Male llamas could be saddled with heavy loads. Females provided meat and milk. People used the wool and skins from both males and females to make cloth and leather. Vicuñas became modern alpacas. Alpacas are smaller than llamas. Ancient Andeans raised these animals mainly for their long wool, which

Ancient Treats

Sapodilla trees grow wild in the forests of Mexico and Central America. They produce a delicious brown fruit that tastes like pears. They also produce a milky sap called chicle. If you boil chicle to remove the water, you're left with a thick, tasteless, gummy substance. The Maya chewed chicle. It was the world's first chewing gum.

The ancient Olmec, who lived in what is now southern Mexico, were the first people to consume chocolate. Chocolate comes from the beans of cacao trees, which grow wild in Mexico and Central America. The Maya loved a chocolate drink. They roasted and ground cacao beans and mixed them with mashed corn, water, hot chili peppers, and spices. People enjoyed the spicy, bitter drink at room temperature. They also used it as medicine.

Chicle comes from the sap of the sapodilla tree, shown here with fruit hanging off the tree's branches.

Llamas are domesticated animals related to camels. Their wild ancestors are guanacos. Ancient Andean people raised llamas for milk, meat, and wool. Male llamas also carried heavy loads on their backs.

is silkier and straighter than sheep's wool.

Archaeologists think that ancient Andeans also domesticated guinea pigs. Guinea pigs have tasty meat, and ancient Andeans raised them for food. Archaeologists have found guinea pig bones at the site of ancient settlements in Peru, Ecuador, and Argentina. Guinea pigs were probably easy to domesticate. They reproduce rapidly, eat household scraps, and can be raised in pens. People in Central and South America still eat these gifts from ancient agriculture.

Hunter-gatherer people in the Andes ate the tuber, or underground stem, of one plant at least six thousand years ago. The ancient Inca domesticated that plant around 5000 BCE. It was the potato. The Inca had another use for the

potato. They used the time needed to boil a potato as a measure of time.

The invention of agriculture helped the Inca establish a great empire, which appeared in the 1400s CE. They built irrigation canals to bring water to dry areas. In hilly areas, Incan farmers cut terraces into the slopes. The terraces gave farmers flat surfaces for planting crops. Terraces also helped keep soil from washing away during rainstorms.

"Every now and then was handed to him a golden pitcher filled with a kind of liquor made from the cacao, which is of a very exciting nature."

—Bernal Díaz del Castillo, Spanish soldier and historian, describing a chocolate drink, 1632

By cutting terraces into hillsides, ancient and modern farmers can create flat growing surfaces. The terraces below were cut by ancient farmers in the Incan city of Machu Picchu in what is now Peru.

CHAPTER SIX
Ancient Greece

A ncient Greek civilization reached its peak from about 500 to 336 BCE. During this time, the ancient Greeks made lasting contributions to science, art, and philosophy. Greek architects designed imposing temples and public buildings. Greek playwrights penned thought-provoking tragedies and comedies. Ancient Greek city-states established some of the world's first democratic governments. And like people in every society, they created their own systems for raising, processing, and distributing food.

Greece is mostly surrounded by water. The Aegean Sea sits to the east of Greece. The Ionian Sea is to the west. The Sea of Crete is to the south. All these waters are arms of the larger Mediterranean Sea. Much of Greece is made up of large and small islands. With so much water all around them, the ancient Greeks naturally looked to the sea for food. They ate lots of fish and shellfish.

The ancient Greeks were also farmers. But Greece is rugged, rocky, and hilly. Much of the land is not good for farming. On suitable land, the ancient Greeks built small

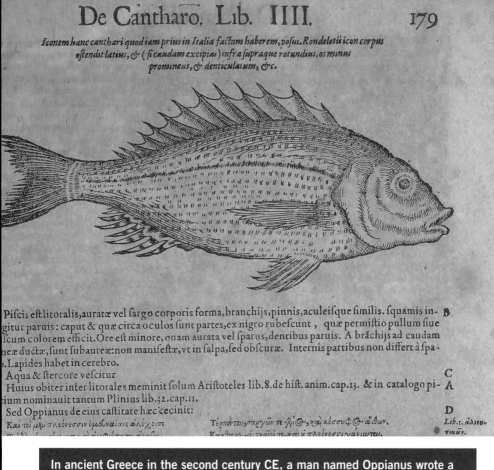

*Iconem hanc canthari quod iam prius in Italia factam haberem, posui. Rondeletii icon corpus
ostendit latius, & (si caudam excipias) infra supraque rotundius, os minus
prominens, & denticulatum, &c.*

Piscis est litoralis, auratæ vel sargo corporis forma, branchijs, pinnis, aculeisque similis. squamis in- **B**
gitur paruis: caput & quæ circa oculos sunt partes, ex nigro rubescunt, quæ permistio pullum siue
scum colorem efficit. Ore est minore, quam aurata vel sparus, dentibus paruis. A brachijs ad caudam
neæ ductæ, sunt subaureæ: non manifestæ, vt in salpa, sed obscuræ. Internis partibus non differt à spa-
b. Lapides habet in cerebro.
Aqua & stercore vescitur.
Huius obiter inter litorales meminit solum Aristoteles lib. 8. de hist. anim. cap. 13. & in catalogo pi- **C A**
sium nominauit tantum Plinius lib. 32. cap. 11.
Sed Oppianus de eius castitate hæc cecinit: **D**

Καὶ τοί μεν πλεόνεσσιν ὁμοῦναίαις ἀλόχοισι   Τέρπον ταις σαργῶν τε ῤυ̃ Θ̃, καὶ κόσου Φ Θ̃ αίθων.   *Lib. i. ἁλιευ-*
                                                Καὶ θν̓ραι οι τγ̃αίοι τε ὐ ω̃ ὰ π λεόνεσσι ναννυντω.   *τικῶν.*

---

farms. The ancient Greeks also imported a lot of food from neighboring lands.

Laertes's Farm

The *Odyssey* is a long poem written around 700 BCE by Homer, an ancient Greek writer. Its hero is Ulysses. Ulysses tries to return home to the Greek island of Ithaca after the Trojan War (which might have taken place around 1200 BCE). Along the way, he has many adventures.

> "There is the place where his fruit trees are grown tall and flourish, pear trees and pomegranate trees and the flourishing olive."
>
> —Homer, The *Odyssey*, 700s BCE

Besides being a beautiful poem, The *Odyssey* tells us a lot about agriculture in ancient Greece. Ulysses wants to return to the farm of his father, Laertes. Homer says that Laertes fertilized the soil with manure and irrigated his fields. He raised a variety of crops that kept him and his workers busy all year. They reaped and threshed wheat and barley in early summer. They picked pears, figs, and other fruit in June, July, and August. In August and September, they harvested grapes and produced wine. Then they planted the next season's wheat. In between all these activities, the workers picked vegetables, ground grain into flour, and performed other farm chores.

Irrigation Systems

Greece has no big river like the Nile in Egypt to provide water for large irrigation projects. So farmers in ancient Greece relied on small irrigation systems. They dammed and diverted streams and springs to bring water to their fields. They hoisted water from wells and poured it into storage tanks or irrigation channels.

Ancient Greek farmers used shadoofs to move water more easily. Another helpful device was the *saqiya*, invented in ancient Persia (modern-day Iran). This machine is sometimes called the Persian water wheel. The saqiya used a series of buckets attached to a rope to lift water from a well or other source. The rope was attached to a wooden wheel. An ox or

These grinding stones come from the island of Syros, southeast of Greece. The mechanical grain mill, invented in ancient Greece, made grinding grain much easier.

camel walked in a circle, rotating the wheel. As the buckets dipped into the water and filled up, they were pulled up by the wheel to pour into an irrigation channel.

In the 200s BCE, the Greek engineer Archimedes of Syracuse made an even better water-hoisting machine. This device was called an Archimedes screw. It consisted of a hollow tube with a big screw inside. The bottom of the tube sat in the water. With the device propped at an angle, a worker turned a crank to operate the screw. As the crank rotated, water trapped in the threads of the screw rose higher and higher until it spilled out of the top of the tube.

Milling Grain

For thousands of years, ancient people ground grain into flour by

Ancient Bakeries

The Greeks were the master bakers of the ancient world. They made bread from different kinds of flour, including wheat, barley, and rye flour. Athenaeus, a Greek writer who lived around 200 CE, compiled a list of more than seventy different kinds of bread made in ancient Greece. In addition to bread, ancient Greek bakeries sold cakes and pastries made with oat flour, honey, cream, dried fruits, and nuts. Archaeologists think that the ancient Greeks made the first cheesecake. Athletes in the early Olympic Games ate it to boost their strength.

hand. They crushed it between two small stones or in a mortar and pestle—a bowl and heavy club. It was hard work, and only a handful of grain could be ground at a time. That began to change in ancient Greece around 100 BCE.

Instead of working with handheld mortars and pestles, farmers took their grain to mills. Large amounts of grain were placed between two big flat stones called millstones. Some stones were 2 or 3 feet (0.6 to 0.9 m) wide. A wooden shaft was attached to the top stone so it could be turned. People or animals turned the stones by walking in a circle. Some Greek mills operated on waterpower. Their millstones were attached to a waterwheel, which sat in a river and turned with the current. A commercial mill could grind more grain in an hour than several people with hand tools could do in a whole day.

CHAPTER SEVEN

Ancient Rome

N omadic people called the Latins started grazing herds of sheep in central Italy around 2000 BCE. By 750 BCE, the Latins had settled into permanent farming villages. One village grew into the city of Rome. The Romans conquered other groups on the Italian Peninsula. They established a republic, a government of elected officials, in 509 BCE. In the first century BCE, Roman leaders fought among themselves for power. In 27 BCE, Octavian, the adopted son of dictator Julius Caesar, took complete control of the Roman government. He declared himself emperor of Rome. Eventually, the Roman Empire conquered and colonized a lot of territory around the Mediterranean Sea, from Britain through Europe to northern Africa and the Middle East.

Roman Farmers

The Italian Peninsula has fertile farmland along its many river

valleys. Ancient Roman farmers grew olives, grapes, wheat, and other fruits and vegetables. They used tools, seeds, and agricultural technology developed earlier throughout the Mediterranean. These included irrigation systems and ox-drawn plows.

Roman farmers also invented agricultural techniques of their own. For instance, they developed a form of crop rotation similar to what modern farmers use. The Romans left half of every field fallow each year. The soil in this uncultivated land stored up nutrients from decayed plant matter and animal droppings and moisture from rain and humidity. The soil became more fertile for the next planting.

This sarcophagus comes from ancient Rome and dates to the third century CE. The sarcophagus shows Romans harvesting grapes for making wine.

AGRICULTURE THROUGH THE AGES

The Romans also rotated crops from field to field. One year they would plant wheat, which robbed the soil of nitrogen. The next year, they would plant legumes such as beans, which restored nitrogen and enriched the soil.

New Harvesting Machines

Cutting stalks of wheat and other grains at harvesttime is called reaping. Throughout the ancient world, farmers used scythes for reaping. A scythe has a long, curved blade and a long wooden handle. Reaping grain with a scythe is slow, hard work.

In the first century CE, farmers in the Roman Empire area known as Gaul (which spread across modern-day France and parts of adjacent countries) devised a machine to make reaping easier. A *vallus* was a two-wheeled, boxlike cart with one end open. The box contained a row of sharp metal blades. A donkey pushed the cart forward through a field of grain, while a laborer steered the cart and directed the stalks into the blades. When the blades cut the stalks, the grain fell into the cart. The vallus saved a lot of labor. Ancient Romans also built a larger version of the vallus, a carpentum.

Keeping Cool

The Romans loved to eat flavored and sweetened ices for dessert. They also loved iced drinks. They cooled wine and fruit juices before drinking them. The ancient Roman drink cooler worked just like a modern ice bucket. The cooler consisted of two pottery jars, one inside the other. The inner jar held wine or another beverage. The outer jar held ice or snow, which cooled the contents of the inner jar. Romans also put chips of ice and

These circles of stone near Rome are all that remain of ancient grain containers. In ancient times, people filled the containers with grain to be ground into flour.

scoops of snow into their glasses to keep drinks chilled.

The Romans also used ice for cold baths in summer, to preserve fish, and to keep other food from spoiling. But Italy and many other parts of the Roman Empire had hot summers. Winters were not very cold. Where did the ancient Romans get snow and ice? They transported it on the backs of mules from snow-covered mountain peaks. When ice merchants reached the city, they sold some of the supply to snow and ice shops, which sold to consumers.

Some of the ice went into storage in icehouses. These were underground pits, sometimes more than 30 feet

(9 m) deep. The cool underground temperatures helped keep the ice from melting. A layer of straw, grass, or leaves sealed the pit opening and served as insulation. It kept cool air inside the pit and warm air out. Ice kept in underground pits could stay frozen for many months.

"Our minds are like our stomachs; they are whetted [stimulated] by the change of their food, and variety supplies both with fresh appetite."

—Marcus Fabius Quintilian, Roman orator, first century CE

Salt of the Earth

Humans and other animals need to eat small quantities of sodium chloride, or salt, to stay healthy. Ancient peoples not only ate salted foods but also used salt to process and preserve foods. Salt kept fish and meat from spoiling. It was used to make cheese and pickle vegetables. Farmers fed salt to their livestock.

Salt comes from underground rock deposits. It can also be made by allowing sea water to evaporate, leaving salt behind. Many places were named for the salt that was mined or processed there. For instance, the name Salzburg (a city in Austria) means "salt town" in German. *Hals* is the ancient Greek word for salt, and the cities of Halle, Belgium, and Halluin, France, were both named for their salt-processing facilities.

Some ancient trading routes were called salt roads. Traders traveled along these roads with blocks of salt carried on the backs of camels, donkeys, and mules. One salt road extended from salt deposits in modern-day Ethiopia to markets in ancient Egypt and Rome. At markets, merchants sold salt in blocks, lumps, cakes, and sheets.

Salt was so important that ancient peoples even used

Wealthy ancient Romans loved to drink and dine. This wall painting from the city of Pompeii shows wealthy Romans at a banquet. They recline while servants attend them.

pieces of salt as money. The ancient Roman government paid soldiers partly in salt. The payment was called a *salarium* (*sal* is the Latin word for salt). That's the origin of our modern word *salary*, which means "a worker's pay." You might have heard someone remark, "They're not worth their salt." That's another way of saying, "They're not worth the money they are paid."

After the Ancients

Ancient societies rose and fell. Often ancient groups grew politically or economically weak and stronger groups conquered them. But even after an ancient culture died out, its technology often remained. Conquering groups built on the knowledge of conquered peoples to further develop technology.

The Western Roman Empire fell to invaders in 476 CE. Although the eastern half of the empire continued to flourish for centuries as the Byzantine Empire, western Europe entered the Middle Ages (about 500 to 1300). The Western Roman Empire slowly broke up into smaller countries. But farmers continued to use and improve agricultural techniques developed by ancient peoples. For instance, European farmers developed a three-field system of crop rotation based on the Roman system. They left one field fallow each year and grew different crops on the other two. This system restored nutrients to the soil but also kept plenty of land cultivated.

European farmers also figured out how to hitch horses to plows during the Middle Ages. Horses could pull plows much

During the Middle Ages, European farmers improved some tools and techniques. But they continued to cut grain by hand, as in this illustration from the fourteenth century CE.

faster than oxen. They enabled European farmers to plow more land, plant more seeds, and grow more food. European farmers continued to breed plants and livestock to produce desirable traits in their offspring. Farmers in northwestern France bred Guernsey cows, which produce a lot of butterfat-rich milk. People use butterfat to make butter.

Expanding Food Horizons

In the 1300s, Europe entered the Renaissance, a time of renewed interest in ancient Greek and Roman art, learning, and culture. European sailors began to explore the world and discover new lands during the Renaissance. This period is often called the Golden Age of Discovery. In 1492 Italian explorer Christopher

Columbus set out across the Atlantic Ocean by ship. He believed that by sailing west around the world, he would reach the Pacific Ocean and Asia.

Columbus was right. One could reach Asia by sailing west from Europe. But Columbus didn't realize that a huge landmass sat between the Atlantic and Pacific Oceans. That landmass consisted of North, Central, and South America. Columbus had arrived at what Europeans later called the New World. Of course, the land was not new to the millions of ancient Americans who called it home. It was not even new to Europeans! Many historians believe that Viking explorers under Leif Erikson visited North America nearly five hundred years earlier.

But after the arrival of Columbus, more European explorers visited the Americas. Settlers and soldiers also arrived to conquer, claim, and colonize various American territories for Spain, France, England, Holland, and other European nations. The newcomers arrived in America hoping to find gold, silver, and other riches—and some of them did. But the Europeans also found something unexpected. They discovered a host of foods developed by Indigenous Americans that were unknown in Europe. These foods included corn, potatoes, chili peppers, tomatoes, bananas, pineapples, peanuts, chocolate, vanilla beans, and avocados.

Merchants began to ship some of these foods back to Europe, where consumers were excited by the new treats. These foods changed European agriculture. Certain American foods, such as tomatoes and potatoes, grew well in Europe. They became important food staples in European cuisine. Other American foods, such as pineapples, grew only in warm, wet tropical places. To obtain more of these

63

foods, European planters began to grow them in their tropical colonies in Asia, Africa, and America.

Indigenous Americans also introduced European explorers and settlers to tobacco. The product caught on quickly in Europe. Tobacco contains nicotine, which is highly addictive. Once people start to smoke, it is very difficult to stop. Some European farmers began to grow tobacco. But the best tobacco came from Virginia in the present-day United States. In the early 1600s, an English colonist named John Rolfe began growing tobacco in Virginia and shipping it to England.

Big Leaps Forward

For thousands of years, farmers did most of their work by hand. At planting time, they walked along their furrows, scattering seeds of grain. At harvesttime, they cut grain with scythes. Horses and other animals helped. But farmers had little in the way of mechanical equipment.

That changed in the 1700s. Then inventors began to build mechanized farm equipment. Jethro Tull of England invented a mechanical seed drill. This machine dug small trenches in soil and deposited seeds in the trenches. The machine replaced the earlier technique of scattering seeds by hand. The drill ensured that seeds ended up where farmers wanted them, and it reduced waste from unevenly planted seeds. But Tull wasn't the first person to invent a device like this. If Tull read Chinese history, he would have found that ancient farmers there had used a similar device in the second century BCE.

In the United States, Eli Whitney invented the cotton gin in 1793. This machine separated cotton fibers from cotton seeds.

Cyrus McCormick's reaper (above), invented in the 1830s, was similar to the ancient Roman vallus. The reaper cut stalks of grain mechanically. People no longer had to use scythes and sickles to cut grain by hand.

It produced cotton fibers much faster than separating the seeds by hand. Able to process cotton faster, farmers grew more and more. Cotton became a leading crop in the southern United States. The cotton gin helped launch the Industrial Revolution in America, a dramatic change to mechanized society which first began in Great Britain.

Unfortunately, the cotton gin did not decrease the need for enslaved Africans on cotton plantations. As demand for cotton grew, so did reliance on the work of enslaved Africans. Many enslaved people in parts of the southern United States were freed by the Emancipation Proclamation on January 1, 1863. Enslavement was completely abolished in the United States with the ratification of the Thirteenth Amendment to the US Constitution on December 6, 1865.

Another important invention was the mechanical reaper. Invented by American Cyrus McCormick in the 1830s, it mechanized all the harvesting tasks that farmers previously did by hand. Was McCormick inspired by ancient Rome's vallus, an early form of a mechanical harvester? In 1837, American John Deere invented the steel plow. This plow turned the soil much more easily and cleanly than earlier iron or wooden plows.

Powering Up

Farmers continued to use horses, oxen, and other animals to power their farm equipment through the 1700s and into the 1800s. But that began to change in the nineteenth century with the arrival of gasoline engines. Farmers began to use gasoline-powered tractors to pull plows, reapers, and other farm machinery.

In the twentieth century, farms became more and more mechanized. Farmers bought electric cow-milking machines and electric irrigation pumps. Agricultural companies developed new chemical fertilizers, insecticides, and weed killers. The breeding of plants and animals became more specialized and scientific. This time period is sometimes called the Green Revolution. In India, China, and other parts of the world, the Green Revolution prevented famine, a lack of food so serious that people die or become sick.

The Biggest and the Best?

By the mid–1900s, farming had become big business around the world. Big corporations set up giant farming operations covering hundreds of thousands of acres of land. These agribusinesses

borrowed techniques from factories to make their farming operations more efficient. Some big farms focused on growing one crop, such as corn. Others raised pigs, chickens, or other livestock in special buildings. Farm managers gave animals drugs to keep them healthy and to make them grow larger and faster.

At first glance, agribusiness seems to have paid off for the United States. In the twenty-first century, US food supplies seem endless. Agribusinesses produce vast amounts of crops and raise millions of animals. At US supermarkets, consumers can choose from thousands of fruits, vegetables, meats, fish, dairy products, and packaged foods. The results of modern agribusiness are impressive. Without it, fewer foods would be on those shelves and the prices would be higher.

But some people worry about the negative effects of modern agribusiness. Chemical fertilizers help improve farm yields. But they can also pollute lakes and rivers. Chemical insecticides and weed killers are effective in protecting plants from bugs and weeds that harm crops. But they can also leave potentially harmful residues that pose a danger to the health of animals and even people. Scientists have evidence that chemicals used to boost the growth of farm animals might also damage the health of consumers. Agribusiness often involves growing a single crop on large farm—a practice called monoculture. This practice has drawbacks. It can leave the crop more vulnerable to diseases that wipe out an entire harvest.

An Old Approach

Farmers in the 1950s and 1960s began rediscovering and embracing more and more ancient farming technology. Those

67

At this organic farm near Lambourn, England, chickens roam freely outdoors. They eat healthy feed with no chemical additives.

techniques became known as organic farming and sustainable agriculture. One of the most important is sustainable agriculture. This approach strives to meet our food and textile needs today without endangering the ability of future generations to meet their own needs. For example, that may involve using more natural ways of fertilizing crops and protecting them from pests. Sustainable farming is new to modern farming, but it's really very old. In ancient times, all farmers were sustainable farmers. They used manure to fertilize crops. They used chrysanthemums and praying mantises to control pests naturally. They rotated crops to restore nutrients to the soil and ensure future crops could be grown. They used cover crops to prevent soil erosion and keep the soil healthy.

Other new approaches to agriculture and food production are gaining in popularity. Organic farmers use animal manure as fertilizer, for instance. They use natural pest control rather than synthetic chemicals. Remember how people in ancient China

used aquaculture? That technology for farming fish and growing plants in water also is popular today. We call it hydroponics and aquaponics. Another ancient agriculture technology has taken root in the twenty-first century under the name regenerative agriculture. It involves ways of preserving the soil and environment used thousands of years ago. This includes no-till or reduced till farming. Instead of plowing entire fields and disturbing all the soil, farmers plant seeds directly into unplowed soil, leaving the healthy soil in place.

Past and Present

Of course, modern society could not exist if we completely returned to the days of ancient farming, let alone hunting and gathering. Farmers worldwide will need to raise enough food to feed almost nine billion people by 2030. When agriculture first emerged, there were barely fifteen million mouths to feed. And most people are happy to buy their food at a supermarket rather than raise it themselves.

But the ancient farming life did have its benefits. People produced nutritious food with their own hands. They were resourceful and found clever ways to overcome difficulties. They knew how to fish and care for animals. They knew which plants were edible. In short, they lived sustainable and were self-sufficient, needing little to no outside help to meet basic needs.

Marcus Tullius Cicero, an ancient Roman orator, knew the value of that life. He wrote, "For of all gainful professions, nothing is better, nothing more pleasing, nothing more delightful, nothing better becomes a well-bred [person] than agriculture." Certainly many ancient farmers—and most modern ones—would agree.

TIMELINE

ca. 400,000 BCE   People in Europe first use fire to cook food.

ca. 14,000 BCE   People in Japan make pottery vessels.

ca. 11,000 BCE   The last ice age ends. As temperatures rise, stands of wild wheat grow in the Fertile Crescent in the Middle East.

ca. 7000 BCE   People in ancient China domesticate millet.

ca. 5000 BCE   People in ancient Scandinavia invent barbed fishhooks. People in ancient Bolivia domesticate potatoes.

ca. 3500 BCE   People in ancient Mesopotamia invent the potter's wheel.

ca. 3000 BCE   People in ancient China begin eating with chopsticks.

ca. 2500 BCE   Ancient Egyptians build a dam across the Nile River to create an artificial lake. Ancient Egyptians begin raising bees.

ca. 2300 BCE   Ancient Egyptians build a canal to Lake Moeris to store excess water from the Nile River.

ca. 1700 BCE   A Babylonian writer carves a series of recipes on two clay tablets.

ca. 800 BCE   Ancient Chinese farmers begin planting rice in paddies.

ca. 700 BCE   Ancient Greek farmers domesticate olive trees. Greek poet Homer writes *The Odyssey*, which describes Laertes's farm.

200s BCE   The ancient Greek mathematician Archimedes invents the Archimedes screw, a kind of water pump.

ca. 100 BCE   Professional millers begin to grind grain with big millstones.

ca. 100	Chinese farmers start using dried chrysanthemums to kill insects on vegetable plants. Farmers in Gaul invent the vallus for cutting stalks of grain.
ca. 300	People in ancient Japan and ancient India learn to make silk.
ca. 550	Emperor Justinian I of the Eastern Roman Empire sends spies to China to learn the secrets of silk making.
1793	US inventor Eli Whitney invents the cotton gin.
1830s	US inventor Cyrus McCormick invents a mechanical reaper.
1837	US inventor John Deere invents the steel plow.
1980s	Professor Daniel Fisher shows that ancient hunter-gatherers might have used underwater caching to keep meat from spoiling.
1994	Researchers at the University of Pennsylvania Museum find the oldest known wine jars. Dating from 5400 to 5000 BCE, the jars come from northern Iran.
2004	Other researchers at the University of Pennsylvania Museum of Archaeology and Anthropology find ancient liquor jars dating from 7000 to 6600 BCE. The jars had contained a fruity cocktail.
2013	Researchers at the Hawaii Space Exploration Analog and Simulation habitat experiment with growing food through hydroponics in a simulated non-Earth environment.
2016	Astronaut Scott Kelly takes a Valentine's Day photograph of a bouquet of zinnias grown on the International Space Station.
2021	Scientists successfully gather two harvests of red and green peppers grown on the International Space Station.

GLOSSARY

agriculture: the science or occupation of growing crops and raising animals to get food and other products

aquaculture: raising fish, shellfish, or edible sea plants in an artificial environment

archaeologist: a scientist who studies the remains of past human cultures

artifact: a human-made object, especially one characteristic of a certain group or a historical period

bacteria: microscopic organisms that might be helpful or harmful to humans

biological pest control: using living things and natural substances to kill insects and pests that harm crops

breed: to mate plants or animals with certain traits to produce offspring with those traits

city-state: a self-governing state consisting of a city and surrounding territory

cultivate: to prepare farmland and grow crops

domestication: the adaptation of a plant or animal from a wild or natural state (as by selective breeding) to life in close association with humans

drought: a long period of little or no rainfall

excavate: to dig into the earth, especially to search for ancient remains or artifacts

fermentation: a chemical change in a substance caused by living organisms such as yeast or bacteria. People use fermentation to make wine, beer, cheese, bread, and other foods.

fertilizer: a substance added to the soil to help plants grow

harvest: to gather crops at the end of the growing season

hunter-gatherers: people who get food primarily by hunting, fishing, and gathering wild plants

irrigation: systems and tools for supplying crops with water

kiln: a large oven or furnace used for hardening pottery or bricks

nutrients: substances in food or soil, such as vitamins or minerals, that provide nourishment to animals or plants

organic farming: farming without using human-made chemicals to kill weeds, kill insects, or fertilize the soil

puddling: flooding fields to grow rice

reap: to cut (as grain) or clear (as a field) with a sickle, scythe, or machine

scavenger: an animal that feeds on the remains of animals that have already been killed or died naturally

slash-and-burn agriculture: chopping down and burning trees on a plot of ground and then planting crops in the cleared land

surplus: the amount more than what is required or necessary

thresh: to separate seed from a harvested plant especially by using a machine or tool

yield: the amount or quantity produced or returned

SOURCE NOTES

27   "Again you will . . . enjoy their fruit.": Jeremiah 31:5 (New International Version).

49   "Every now and . . . very exciting nature.": Bernal Díaz del Castillo, *The Memoirs of the Conquistador Bernal Diaz del Castillo*, vol 1 (London: J. Hatchard and Son, 1844), 230.

52   "There is the . . . the flourishing olive.": Homer, *The Odyssey of Homer*, trans. Richmond Lattimore (New York: HarperCollins, 1999), 114.

59   "Our minds are . . . with fresh appetite.": Tryon Edwards, *A Dictionary of Thoughts* (Detroit: F. B. Dickerson, 1908), 348.

69   "For of all gainful . . . well-bred [person] than agriculture.": Susan Ratcliffe, ed. "Cicero." Oxford Reference, accessed March 21, 2023, https://www.oxfordreference.com /display/10.1093/acref/9780191826719.001.0001/q-oro-ed4 -00003011;jsessionid=5A5C36412EDE51AEBAEE35A9BAC66754.

SELECTED BIBLIOGRAPHY

Diamond, Jared. *Guns, Germs, and Steel: The Fates of Human Societies*. New York: W. W. Norton, 1999.

Fagan, Brian M., ed. *Discovery! Unearthing the New Treasures of Archaeology*. London: Thames and Hudson, 2007.

———. *The Seventy Great Inventions of the Ancient World*. London: Thames and Hudson, 2004.

Ferdández-Armesto, Felipe. *Near a Thousand Tables: A History of Food*. New York: Free Press, 2002.

Freedman, Paul, ed. *Food: The History of Taste*. Berkeley: University of California Press, 2007.

Hanson, Victor Davis. *The Other Greeks: The Family Farm and the Agrarian Roots of Western Civilization*. New York: Free Press, 1995.

James, Peter, and Nick Thorpe. *Ancient Inventions*. New York: Ballantine Books, 1994.

Kurlansky, Mark. *Choice Cuts: A Savory Selection of Food Writing from around the World and throughout History*. New York: Ballantine Books, 2002.

Salzberg, Hugh W. *From Caveman to Chemist*. Washington, DC: American Chemical Society, 1991.

Smith, Bruce D. *The Emergence of Agriculture*. New York: Scientific American Library, 1995.

Toussaint-Samat, Maguelonne. *A History of Food*. Cambridge, MA: Blackwell Reference, 1993.

Turner, Jack. *Spice: The History of Temptation*. New York: Alfred A. Knopf, 2004.

Visser, Margaret. *Much Depends on Dinner*. New York: Grove, 1986.

FURTHER READING

Books

Hirsch, Rebecca E. *Where Have All the Bees Gone? Pollinators in Crisis*. Minneapolis: Twenty-First Century Books, 2020.
Bees play an essential role in growing everything from cucumbers to coffee. But the number of bees around the world is on the decline. Learn about the many species of bees on Earth and how you can help protect them.

Kimmerer, Robin Wall, and Monique Gray Smith. *Braiding Sweetgrass for Young Adults*. Minneapolis: Zest Books, 2022.
Drawing from her experiences as an Indigenous scientist, Robin Wall Kimmerer demonstrates how living things at all levels work together to provide us with gifts and knowledge. Discover how Indigenous wisdom, ancient agricultural practices, and scientific knowledge can teach us to better appreciate the world and our place in it.

McCarty, Joellen, ed. *The Industrial Food Complex*. New York: Greenhaven, 2020.
Everyone relies on the food industry in their daily lives. But as the contributions of industrialized agriculture to animal cruelty, human exploitation, and climate change are becoming clearer, many people are questioning whether the benefits are worth the costs. Learn about the various viewpoints on the issue as well as the possible solutions.

Pollan, Michael. *The Botany of Desire. Young Readers Edition*. New York: Rocky Pond Books, 2023.
Food writer Michael Pollan explores the history of our relationship with plants, how we domesticated them, and the ways humans and plants benefit from each other. Discover the symbiotic relationships between humans and the plants we grow.

Woods, Michael, and Mary B. Woods. *Machines through the Ages: From Furnaces to Factories*. Minneapolis: Twenty-First Century Books, 2024.
All machines are based on six simple machines: the lever, the wheel and axle, the inclined plane, the pulley, the wedge, and the screw. Discover how ancient civilizations around the world used simple machines to build everything from basic tools to the great wonders of the ancient world.

Websites

The Food Timeline
  https://www.foodtimeline.org
  This site, managed by Virginia Tech University, follows the history
  of food from prehistoric humanity to the modern day. Explore
  hundreds of recipes covering over nineteen thousand years of
  culinary history.

History of Potatoes
  http://whatscookingamerica.net/History/PotatoHistory.htm
  This site traces the history of the potato, from its origins in ancient
  South America to modern dinner tables. You'll also find links to
  recipes and even famous quotes about potatoes.

Impact of Sustainable Agriculture and Farming Practices
  https://www.worldwildlife.org/industries/sustainable-agriculture
  Agriculture takes up more and more space on Earth as the human
  population grows. But some people are trying to grow more food
  in less space. Learn about the sustainable practices farmers and
  scientists are exploring through this site by the World Wildlife
  Fund.

Pearls
  https://www.amnh.org/exhibitions/pearls
  Pearls were prized in ancient times, just as they are in modern
  times. This website from the American Museum of Natural History
  explains how oysters make pearls and how people interfere with
  nature to find and make even more pearls.

INDEX

ABOUT THE AUTHORS

Michael Woods is a science and medical journalist in Washington, DC. He has won many national writing awards. Mary B. Woods is a school librarian. Their past books include the fifteen–volume *Disasters Up Close* series and many titles in the *Seven Wonders* series. The Woodses have four children. When not writing, reading, or enjoying their seven grandchildren, the Woodses travel to gather material for future books.

PHOTO ACKNOWLEDGMENTS